The Ultimate Hotel Development Guide

For Non-Hotel Developers

Everything a community leader or person looking to develop a new hotel will need to get the project done!

Thank you to all the wonderful people throughout my career that have allowed me to grow and learn!

About the Author:

Miss Junker offers nearly 20 years of hospitality industry experience. From her beginning in the industry as a banquet server at a full-service hotel in downtown Green Bay, Wisconsin, to overseeing that very property as the manager in a couple of years. Jessica moved on to work as a Director of Sales at a Residence Inn by Marriott, Area Director of Sales with Interstate Hotels, and Regional Director of Sales and Marketing with Archon Hospitality (a Goldman Sachs Company)/Pillar Hotels working on the Sales, Marketing, and Revenue Management of anywhere between 15 and 52 hotels with every major and not so major brand in the country. After learning everything she felt she needed about running a hotel, she set her sights on what happens before a hotel is built and worked in many separate executive roles with-in an up-and-

coming hotel franchise. Miss Junker offers hands-on, expert knowledge in hotel operations, sales, marketing, training, contracting, development, construction, really all things hotels. She gained this knowledge from industry leaders like Marriott, Hilton, InterContinental Hotels Group, Choice Hotels, TMI Hospitality, Interstate Hotels, Pillar Hotels & Resorts, Cobblestone Hotels, Wyndham Hotels & Resorts, and many more.

The Ultimate

Guide

Have you been pounding your head against the wall wondering if you will ever be able to bring a new hotel development into your community? Whether you are an Investor, City Administrator, Mayor, Economic Development Director, or anyone in the business of growing the economy of communities across the United States, the task can be daunting. From developers that stretch the truth to brands that make promises, they can never keep. The Hotel Development process can go on for months and even years without any real movement.

This book is here for you! The Ultimate Hotel Development Guide offers a detailed, step-by-step guide to help you through the process and ensure you are not taken for a ride that leads to nothing!

Thank you for taking the time to read The Ultimate Hotel Development Guide. All the templates located in this book can be downloaded for use by visiting www.TheUltimateHotelDevelopmentGuide.com

In addition, if you are looking to have a Comprehensive Hotel Market Feasibility Study conducted in your community, I can be reached at:

Jessica Junker

920-740-1647

j.junker@coredistinctiongroup.com

www.coredistinctiongroup.com

Also, if you are looking for a Multi-Family, Single-Family, or Senior Housing Feasibility Study, I can be reached at:

Jessica Junker

920-740-1647

jessica@housing-advisors.com

www.housing-advisors.com

Chapter One

HOW DOES A HOTEL IMPACT YOUR COMMUNITY?

HOW DOES A HOTEL IMPACT YOUR COMMUNITY?

When looking at the impact of a hotel, there are many things to consider.

How will its location impact other businesses?

How will a new hotel being built affect the employee pool?

The most important impact in this stage of your process is what you can expect as an economic impact. This factor is important when looking to purchase a Comprehensive Hotel Market Feasibility Study. In most cases, the governing entity looking to purchase a study wants to ensure a new hotel will have a positive impact on their community. These entities as well as hotel developers, brands, and management companies also want to ensure potential project offers a positive return on investment. Let us go over the economic impact of a new hotel being built in a community.

Direct Impact

When considering the direct economic impact of a hotel, you need to consider the hotel itself. The actual revenue brought in by the hotel. The jobs it creates. The operating costs paid to the local community. These things can range from the purchase of donuts from the local bakery every morning to utilities the hotel pays each month. Or the taxes generated to the community. These taxes have a local and regional reach. Some communities even take advantage of collecting a local lodging or bed tax, using it to market and attract tourism to their community. You can also consider the jobs created during the construction of the hotel. All these things, large or small, will make an impact on a community in a positive manner (if the hotel is feasible).

Collateral Economic Impact

The secondary impact of building a new hotel in your community is the collateral economic impact. Collateral economic impact affects a community in so many ways that I will simply give you a few examples and let your mind do the rest. When people are able to stay in your community instead of driving to the next, they fill up their gas tank, buy snacks, have dinner at the local restaurant, stop at your local unique boutique to spend a few dollars and so on. They may even catch stop at your local history museum, enjoy a tour and donate. If you sit down and think about the potential impact, it is huge! All these things and more create collateral jobs, revenue, and tax dollars.

The fact is, bringing a hotel into your community will keep travelers in your community. Small and big communities across the country are home to great tourist attractions, fantastic sporting events, social events, and many local companies that have regional and even national offices. These places have visitors daily and when there is no place to stay, these visitors, stay 30 miles or more away. Taking their money with them. They will also not be able to tell their friends and family about the great town they visited last week and all it had to offer. That is a darn shame!

You may be thinking, "Yes, but can you give me some numbers?". Yes, I can!

Throughout the last 4 months or so, I have had many calls and emails from community leaders, hotel owners, hotel investors, bankers, developers, brands, industry strategists, and so on asking what my thoughts are on the current state of the hotel industry and hotel development. Although those conversations are in-depth, my conclusions, when it comes to new hotel development are always the same. When speaking to community leaders and hotel developers looking at beginning the process of conducting a Comprehensive Hotel Market Feasibility Study, I say the same thing. START NOW!

I may be biased but, I believe my reasoning and opinions have some merit. Considering that 75% of our municipality clients have little to no lodging supply in their community, the economic impact of a new, quality hotel can be substantial. Let me explain in more detail.

The average US Hotel Occupancy in 2019 was 66.2% [1]. Great numbers! Additional data shows the average US Hotel Occupancy in 2008 was 59.8% [1] and the average US Hotel Occupancy in 2009 54.6% [1]. Also, the average US Hotel ADR (Average Daily Rate) in 2019 was $131.21 [2] and US Hotel RevPar (Revenue Per Available Room) in 2019 was $86.76 [3].

Now keep in mind that every community is different, the numbers are on a national level and for this exercise only. To understand the direct, brass tax, numbers, or money potential economic impact of a new hotel let's talk about a hypothetical, new build, 50 room hotel in your community.

Based on the data, this hotel would perform as follows (Pre-Covid):

50 rooms at 66.2% Occupancy - 33 rooms sold each day (average)

$131.21 Average Daily Rate (revenue brought in by each room sold)

Total Revenue per day - $4,329.93

The Total Revenue Per Year for this hypothetical hotel would be, $1,580,424.45.

When considering the potential sales tax revenue of this hypothetical hotel, a municipality charging 3% local sales tax, would bring $47,412.73 in additional sales tax revenue per year.

This is not to mention a lodging or bed tax in your community (which I believe all communities should have). This does not account for the collateral economic impact as well. What about real estate taxes?

The average real estate taxes for new hotels this size, based on the communities Core Distinction Group has worked with to conduct Comprehensive Hotel Market Feasibility Studies, I would estimate an average of $60,000. I work in many different states, counties, parishes, towns, cities, and villages. This number varies and is only an estimate.

Again, this information does not account for the collateral economic impact. There are many collateral economic impacts that can be accounted for. As mentioned previously, additional revenue (and usage) from your sewer, water, trash disposal, utilities, and so on. The construction period can also promote additional economic growth. All of these add up and vary.

A more notable collateral economic impact is food or meals. On average, a traveler will spend $42 per day on meals[4]. Your community's new hotel is bringing in 33 new rooms each night. In this case, we will use the average number of people that stay in a hotel room at 1.5. With this data we can assume you have 49.5 additional people, on average, staying in your community (for business or leisure travel). How does that impact the local restaurants and gas stations selling food? Utilizing these numbers for your potential collateral economic impact we can do the math again:

49.5 people spending $42 per day?
$2,079 additional, food collateral revenue per day

49.5 people spending $42 per day for a year?
$758,835 additional, food collateral revenue per year

Based on this information, a municipality charging 3% local sales tax, would bring in:

$22,765.05 additional tax revenue per year

Not to mention the happy business owners capturing that additional collateral revenue! These potential collateral economic impact numbers go on and on. Below area few to take into consideration:

Average Spend on Entertainment[4] - $51 per day

49.5 people spending $51 per day?
$2,524.5 additional, collateral revenue per day

49.5 people spending $51 per day for a year?
$921,442.50 additional, collateral revenue per year

$27,643.27 additional tax revenue per year

Average Spend on Alcohol[4] - $19 per day

49.5 people spending $19 per day?
$940.50 additional, collateral revenue per day

49.5 people spending $19 per day for a year?
$343,282.50 additional, collateral revenue per year

$10,298.48 additional tax revenue per year

Average Spend on Local Transportation[4] - $36 per day

49.5 people spending $36 per day?
$1,782 additional, collateral revenue per day

49.5 people spending $36 per day for a year?
$650,430 additional, collateral revenue per year

$19,512.90 additional tax revenue per year

Average Spend on Tips[4] - $12 per day

49.5 people spending $12 per day?
$594 additional, the economic impact to collateral employees per day

49.5 people spending $12 per day for a year?
$216,810 additional, the economic impact to collateral employees per year

You can figure out the impact on any collateral expenditures but to keep it simple, we will focus on the direct, quantifiable, tax revenue a hotel will bring to a community. Below are the total impacts of each tax collected on a 50 rooms hotel (estimates based on the numbers given earlier):

Hotel Sales Tax Revenue - $47,412.73

Hotel Real Estate Taxes Per Year - $60,000

Total Hotel Direct Tax Revenue - $107,412.73

PER YEAR!

Again, this does not account for the additional collateral impact on sales tax revenue noted throughout this chapter. An additional important factor in this scenario is job creation. A hotel this size is may only create 7 to 10 Full-Time Equivalents (FTEs) but the additional 49.5 people in the community going to your local restaurants and attractions, may have a larger job creation impact.

Now you are probably thinking, "This is all fine and dandy, but this is 2020! WHAT ABOUT COVID?".

1. Source - www.statista.com
2. Source - www.statista.com
3. Source - www.statista.com
4. Source - www.budgetyourtrip.com
5. Source - www.forbes.com

Chapter Two

COVID...COVID...DEMAND

COVID...COVID...DEMAND

When deciding if you should take the plunge, contract a Comprehensive Hotel Feasibility Study, and begin the process of bringing a new hotel into your community, ask yourself this question:

IS THERE DEMAND?

Demand is crucial in deciding to take the first step in the process. As a Hotel Development Consulting Firm, if my company cannot justify the need for a new hotel room if there is no way to find it feasible. Are local employers, attractions, and community members begging you to attract a new hotel? Is your Chamber having to send people to the town or county down the highway for lodging? If these questions are answered with a "YES", you have demand. We will discuss this further in later chapters but that is reason enough to justify the expense of a Comprehensive Hotel Market Feasibility Study. But should you start such a process during or right after a pandemic?

Your mind may be blown but this will not last forever! There are a few points that are important to your decision making in the next year or so:

US Travel Spending is expected to drop by 45% in 2020

US Travel Spending is expected to increase by 37.5% in 2021[5]

In my opinion, these numbers will not reach 45% in 2020 and there will be a faster recovery but that is just my twenty years of Hotel Industry experience. Do the math. Look at your community's economic indicators in 2008, 2009, 2010, 2011, and 2012. How does it look? How dramatic was your recession? How fantastic was your recovery?

In my experience, large cities were the ones hit the hardest during these times. I see it in Hotel Occupancy, Unemployment, Housing, and so on. In my opinion, do not take the word of the reporter reporting on the grave status of a city hundreds, if not thousands of miles from your community. Look at YOUR history.

There are also some important factors to consider when looking at developing a new hotel in certain communities:

1. According to STR Global, it takes a little less than two years to construct an Upscale Midscale, Upper Midscale Hotel and even a Midscale is taking more than a year in the US.[1]
2. Development time on a new hotel can be anywhere between one and three years. Some can take longer.

This information tells us that it can take between two and five or more years from the beginning of the development process to the open date. Should you wait a year or two to start a process that can take more than five years?

Another important piece of the puzzle we have been hearing for the last few months is that communities want to wait to ensure the impact on their potential hotel development does not impact their Comprehensive Hotel Market Feasibility Study results. In my opinion, this is a severe mistake. Let me explain.

I had a client call me begging for help after choosing a competitor to conduct their Comprehensive Hotel Market Feasibility Study. When Covid hit the US like a brick in March, the competitor (who had signed the contract in late February) sent the fee back and said they did not know how to complete a study with this type of situation. Keep in mind the only reason the client did not go with my firm is that we had higher prices. Repeat after me, "YOU GET WHAT YOU PAY FOR, YOU GET WHAT YOU PAY FOR"! These sorts of situations happen often. I can tell you, more than 10% of our revenue, on any given year (sometimes more than 25%) is fixing our competitor's mistakes. Fun fact, the client ends up paying more than they would've if they had just gone with us.

Take the time to review this book and advise. Whether you choose my company or another, choose someone that understands the industry and is not afraid to roll their sleeves up, learn, grow, and do the research! Rant over!

Any company that conducts Comprehensive Hotel Market Feasibility Studies should know the ins and outs of the industry and how to identify need prior to, during, and after COVID. While we are not psychic, we can take past trends into consideration and with proper research, investigate, and analyze any community's need now and into the future.

1- www.hotelnewsnow.com

2 - www.statista.com

Chapter Three

IS THERE ENOUGH NEED
IN THE MARKET?

IS THERE ENOUGH NEED IN THE MARKET?

To say we get this question a lot is an understatement. The thing about this question is we (the HOTEL FEASIBILITY STUDY COMPANY) could not possibly answer that question with an educated answer. We have competitors that will fill your head full of hope and half-truths about the industry. They may even tell you about a community they worked with down the road. The thing about putting out this information is that it tells you NOTHING about your actual market.

Face it, you know more about your community than any consulting firm can tell you when they have not done the research. You have reached out for a reason and by the time you get to the point of actually getting a Comprehensive Hotel Market Feasibility Study, you know you have need (whether you have enough need is the real question). Yes, we have had studies come back without enough need to support a new hotel. The new hotel must make good business sense, or it will eventually be an empty building. No one wants that!

There are many things to consider when deciding to purchase a Comprehensive Hotel Market Feasibility Study. The first and foremost aspect to consider? As discussed in the previous chapter, is there enough need for a new hotel? Need is an all-determining factor that puts a project over the edge to making good business sense. Sure there are other factors like land cost/availability in the area, interest in the market from the industry (as a side note a positive feasibility study is a marketing tool to bring interest), labor costs in the market, competitors, and much more.

The key to all these factors is they are all addressed in the Comprehensive Hotel Market Feasibility Study. Need. Need. Need. We cannot say it enough. A large percentage of people that contact us have already been told for months and even years that there is a need in the market. If that is not the case in your community, find out.

Here one question to ask yourself to make a more educated and money-saving decision:

1. Have community leaders complained about not having a hotel for visitors?

Answer: YES!!!!

Okay, great! Have they complained because they have a tangible need or because they want a hotel to improve the economy? This is key to your process. There is an exceptionally large difference between need and want. A lot of communities want to see a project for jobs and other economic impact reasons. Simply put, if you do not have a quantifiable need, you will end up with an empty building that no one wants.

Answer: NO!!!!

Okay now, if you have not heard from community leaders with need, why are you even reading this book? Do you know that the current hotels/motels are sold out a large percentage of the time? Do you know people are leaving the area for higher quality lodging? Do you see and hear complaints about your current accommodations? I am sure you have your reason to learn about developing a new hotel in your community.

You have the reason, now get some information to back that reason. Ask business leaders what they think of the current accommodations. Ask demand generators where their current guests are staying. Start to build a case to purchase that Comprehensive Hotel Market Feasibility Study.

Believe it or not, I have had many people put so much focus on getting land nailed down or investors in place, they never actually look at the demand or need for a new hotel. If you have a positive Comprehensive Hotel Market Feasibility Study, those things fall into place much easier.

When you can answer this question and still feel it is time to take the next step and gain an understanding of the tools needed when developing a new hotel in your community.

Chapter Four

TOOLS FOR DEVELOPING
A NEW HOTEL

TOOLS FOR DEVELOPING A NEW HOTEL

There are many tools or pieces of the puzzle needed to get a hotel developed in your community. The most important aspect is to have a third-party, Comprehensive Hotel Market Feasibility Study completed for your market. This study is crucial to starting the process and getting your community in front of the other pieces of the puzzle.

There are 8 major tools to bring a new hotel to your community. Let us review them all quickly. All these tools will be explained in more detail in later lessons.

1. HOTEL FEASIBILITY STUDY - Yes that is my main business, but I do many other things. The point is you need a study to get the project started much less done. The only way around getting a study is if you do the project by yourself. No investors, no financing, and so on. You pay for everything!

2. HOTEL DEVELOPER - Unless you are going to develop the project yourself, you will need a HOTEL DEVELOPER to put all the other pieces together and keep the project moving.

3. HOTEL INVESTOR/S - This goes to the previous comment about doing it yourself. Unless you are financially able to build the hotel yourself, you will need a hotel investor or investors.

4. HOTEL GENERAL CONTRACTOR - The hotel general contractor, in most cases will come with another tool (one of the 2-5). The important part to remember, regarding this tool, most commercial contractors can help with this and in most cases, it is not hard to find a hotel general contractor. All that considered, an experienced hotel general contractor will make the process much easier and all commercial contractors are not alike. I highly recommend utilizing a hotel-specific, general contractor.

5. HOTEL BRAND - Most Comprehensive Hotel Market Feasibility Studies will recommend a brand or a scale, but the hard part is getting certain brands to call back. That is where a good hotel developer can help the process.

6. HOTEL MANAGEMENT COMPANY - To follow the hotel brand info, most brands will require an approved, professional hotel management company. Make sure you are working with all parties to ensure you are utilizing a company they trust.

7. LAND - If you do not have land, where are you going to put the hotel? This is a necessary tool. Land can range in size and location but in some cases, there can be more than one option. Not to put even more emphasis on the study but a quality Comprehensive Hotel Market Feasibility Study will recommend land options in your community as well as review the land you are looking at (if needed). You hired the consultant for a reason. Ask for their opinion. If they are experienced, they will give it.

8. INCENTIVES - Depending on the market, in most cases, some sort of incentive is needed. It can be as little as waiving water hook-up fees but most investors, developers, and so on are looking for some sort of incentive. I have seen municipalities offer ridiculous amounts of money due to the lack of lodging in the area and the lost revenue in the community. Every community is different.

Now that you have a simple understanding of the tools you need to get your hotel project completed, here is a checklist to help you get started:

- o I understand how a hotel can impact my community.
- o I understand why my community has need for a new hotel.
- o I understand what tools I need to develop a new hotel in my community.

Chapter Five

HOTEL FEASIBILITY STUDY

HOTEL FEASIBILITY STUDY

There are many companies out there that complete Hotel Feasibility Studies. My company, Core Distinction Group, LLC is the top of the pack (in my opinion of course). If you feel the need to seek out others, there are some important questions you should ask them. I have had community leaders call me for just the price. No interest in our process or why we may be better than a different company for that community. It seems crazy but the price is not always the most important aspect of your process. As stated in an earlier chapter, my company probably has 10 to 25 percent of its contracts each year that are simply re-doing a study a competitor completed. Simply because they did not understand the type of project they were working on or the community did not understand what was needed to get the hotel project done. There are questions that we always recommend asking whether you contact our company or another firm.

Here are those questions:

1. Will the completed study be community-specific? Some Comprehensive Hotel Market Feasibility Study companies utilize regional, state, and even national data in their studies. You want your study to be about your community and possibly a bit of information about any feeder communities sounding your community.

2. Do you have any past 'hands-on' hotel operations experience? Some Comprehensive Hotel Market Feasibility Study companies, believe it or not, have never actually worked in the industry. This is important when understanding where the need comes from as well as having a firm understanding of the operation and operational costs of a new hotel development.

3. How familiar and comfortable are you with the working dynamics of communities around our size? Some Comprehensive Hotel Market Feasibility Study companies do not understand the needs of certain sizes of communities. The

needs of a 3,000 person community are much different than a community of 50,000, 100,0000, or even 1,000,000, and higher. It is extremely important your firm understands this.

4. Will you be coming to visit our community and conduct one-on-one demand generator interviews? Some Comprehensive Hotel Market Feasibility Study companies only do "group" interviews where they speak to many people in the community. Some speak to hoteliers in the community that will only view the potential new hotel as a way for them to lose money. Some will not interview anyone and base everything on the data. One-on-One interviews are crucial when digging into the needs of demand generators in the area. This one-on-one interview, in many cases, can even uncover additional need the demand generator did not realize they had.

5. Will you work closely with a developer/contractor/brand to use accurate development and construction costs? Some Comprehensive Hotel Market Feasibility Study companies use "industry standards" for pricing on construction or even operating costs. This can be detrimental to a project as costs change between brands, size, amenities, and many other factors. Utilizing "industry standards" is not a good option when reviewing a project comprehensively.

6. What happens if early in the process it is found the community cannot support a New hotel? Some Comprehensive Hotel Market Feasibility Study companies charge you even if you do not receive a report. Some companies charge you between 50 and 75 percent and the remainder is not collected if your community does not receive a full Comprehensive Hotel Market Feasibility Study.

7. What will be included in your fee? All
   Comprehensive Hotel Market Feasibility Studies
   should offer the study as well as the financial
   proforma. The fee should also include all the
   firm's expenses. In addition, the fee should be
   given up-front for any follow-up services or
   ongoing services. I have seen companies charge
   over $250 an hour to discuss the product they
   created.

8. What will be the total cost for the comprehensive
   study, a five-year forward-looking Pro-forma, and
   a five-year break-even analysis? Some
   Comprehensive Hotel Market Feasibility Study
   companies have multiple phases and are not
   clear in their pricing. Please ensure you will be
   receiving everything needed to attract new
   hotel development to your community.

9. How long will the study take from contract to completion? Some Comprehensive Hotel Market Feasibility Study companies take up to 3 or even more than 6 months to complete a study. These long wait times will ensure an extreme drop in the momentum of a new hotel project. Take the time to ensure the study will be completed promptly. Ensure the completion date is in the contract.

Asking these questions will ensure you are hiring the right fit for your company. Whether it is my company, Core Distinction Group, or one of our competitors, gaining an understanding of that company by asking the right questions will ensure you have a good partnership for your company.

If you decide to seek out a Hotel Feasibility Study Firm via a Request for Proposal method, try and keep in mind the response you get cannot tell you what the firm is all about. Make sure you speak with each consultant. Get a feel for their personality.

Personally, I will not do much research on a community before they hire my company. When organizations contact me after they have reviewed my proposal and ask about their community, I will tell them as such. I have not been paid yet will not tell them my thoughts on their community before being hired. I believe that honesty is the best medicine and feel like most appreciate that honesty. Even if the person looking to hire my company has given the "elevator speech" on their community. I have not done the research and have not done the work to come to a determination. How could I give an honest answer? In my opinion, if a competing firm answers that question without doing the work, how can you trust the report they will complete for you?

All that said, a good Request for Proposal is essential if you are going to go that route. The following two pages have a simple template you can use to construct a good Hotel Feasibility Study Request for Proposal.

You can also download this and all the other templates in this book at www.theultimatehoteldevelopmentguide.com !

THE COMMUNITY OF COMMUNITY NAME, STATE REQUESTS YOU PARTICIPATE IN THEIR HOTEL FEASIBILITY STUDY PROPOSAL PROCESS BY DEADLINE DATE

THE NAME OF ORGANIZATION IS SEEKING PROPOSALS FROM QUALIFIED HOTEL CONSULTING FIRMS TO PERFORM A FEASIBILITY ANALYSIS WITHIN THEIR COMMUNITY. THE CHOSEN CONSULTANT/COMPANY MUST BE PROFICIENT IN COMMUNITY FACILITATION, POSITIVE ENGAGEMENT, STRONG DATA ANALYSIS, AS WELL AS NOTED INDUSTRY EXPERIENCE AND KNOWLEDGE.

IF YOUR COMPANY WISHES TO BE CONSIDERED FOR THIS PROJECT, PLEASE EMAIL A COPY OF YOUR PROPOSAL TO NAME OF CONTACT AT EMAIL ADDRESS.

ABOUT THE COMMUNITY (MAKE THIS SECTION YOUR ELEVATOR SPEECH ABOUT YOUR COMMUNITY)

SELECTION TIMELINE, REQUIREMENTS AND CRITERIA

SELECTION TIMELINE:

DATE   PROPOSAL SUBMITTED
DATE   PHONE INTERVIEWS OF TOP THREE PROPOSALS
DATE   SELECT FIRM AND ISSUE CONTRACT

EACH PROPOSAL MUST, AT THE MINIMUM OFFER THE FOLLOWING:

- A LIST OF SIMILAR PROJECTS COMPLETED
- A LIST OF REFERENCES
- RESUMES OF PROFESSIONAL STAFF MEMBERS THAT WILL WORK ON THE PROJECT
- NAME OF PERSON TO BE IN CHARGE OF PROJECT
- A DESCRIPTION OF THE FIRM'S PROPOSED PROJECT APPROACH, DEMONSTRATING AN UNDERSTANDING OF THE PROJECT AND ITS INTENDED DELIVERABLES
- A PROJECT SCHEDULE AND TIMELINE FOR COMPLETION
- A DETAILED DESCRIPTION OF COST

THE COMPANY SELECTED WILL BE DONE SO BY THE FOLLOWING CRITERIA:

- BACKGROUND HISTORY AND PERFORMANCE OF THE FIRM
- CAPABILITIES TO PROVIDE REQUIRED SERVICES
- DEMONSTRABLE EXPERIENCE WORKING WITH SIMILAR SIZED COMMUNITIES
- PROJECT MANAGER EXPERIENCE AND QUALIFICATIONS
- STRENGTH AND EXPERIENCE OF ASSIGNED STAFF
- RELATED PROJECT EXPERIENCE
- PROJECT UNDERSTANDING AND APPROACH
- REFERENCES
- FEE PROPOSAL

SCOPE OF WORK

THE STUDY SHOULD ADDRESS THE CURRENT AND PROJECTED MARKET DEMAND FOR THE NUMBER OF ROOMS; TYPE AND DURATION OF HOTEL STAYS IN THE STUDY AREA; THE BUILD-ABILITY OF POTENTIAL SITES; A COMPETITIVENESS ANALYSIS AND ASSESSMENT ON WHAT A HOTEL FACILITY MUST DO TO REACH A BREAKEVEN POINT; AN ECONOMIC FEASIBILITY ANALYSIS, COMPLETE WITH A PROFORMA, SOURCES AND USES, AND AN OPERATING BUDGET FOR A POTENTIAL HOTEL. COMPLETE WITH PROJECTIONS THROUGH YEAR 5 OR LONGER; AND AN APPRAISAL TO ASSIST IN PROJECT FINANCING. PLEASE SEE FOLLOWING IN MORE DETAIL:

MARKET DEMAND ANALYSIS

- FUTURE LODGING & HOSPITALITY DEMAND IN THE MARKET AREA
- REVIEW OF DEMAND GENERATORS
- REVIEW OF STR REPORTS

PROJECT FEASIBILITY STUDY

- PROJECT FEASIBILITY STUDY
- ASSESS THE VIABILITY OF THE PREFERRED HOSPITALITY PRODUCT IN COMMUNITY
- IDENTIFY MARKET CONSTRAINTS
- ESTIMATE OCCUPANCY RATES
- ESTIMATE CAPITAL INVESTMENT REQUIRED AND EXPECTED REVENUE RETURN NEEDED TO ATTRACT ABLE INVESTORS
- ESTIMATE MUNICIPAL ROOM TAX REVENUE

FACILITY RECOMMENDATION

- VIABLE BRANDS
- NUMBER AND MIX OF GUEST ROOMS
- TYPES OF ON-SITE GUEST AMENITIES

FINANCIAL PROJECTIONS

- FINANCIAL PROFORMA THAT CAN BE PROVIDED TO POTENTIAL HOTEL DEVELOPERS, LENDING INSTITUTIONS, MANAGEMENT COMPANIES AND FRANCHISES
- POTENTIAL PROJECTIONS FOR YEAR 1-5 (MINIMUM)
- A BREAKEVEN ANALYSIS

Now that you have a simple template for your Hotel Feasibility Study Request for Proposal, here is a checklist to help you get started:

- o I have reviewed the Hotel Feasibility Study RFP Template.
- o I have completed my market's Hotel Feasibility Study RFP.
- o I have summited my Hotel Feasibility Study RFP to professional firms.
- o I have followed the steps given and contracted with a professional hotel feasibility study firm.

If you are looking for this service, feel free to contact me for more questions:

Jessica Junker

Managing Partner, Core Distinction Group, LLC

920-740-1647

j.junker@coredistinctiongroup.com

www.coredistinctiongroup.com

Chapter Six

YOU HAVE A COMPREHENSIVE HOTEL FEASIBILITY STUDY, NOW WHAT?

YOU HAVE A COMPREHENSIVE HOTEL FEASIBILITY STUDY, NOW WHAT?

Once you have your completed Hotel Feasibility Study in hand, the next step is to get the document as well as the GOOD NEWS in as many hands as possible! The following page offers a template for your press release. Pay attention to the capitalized lettering as that is the wording you will need to change to your information.

Reminder, you can also download this and all the other templates in this book at www.theultimatehoteldevelopmentguide.com !

Here is your HOTEL FEASIBILITY STUDY PRESS RELEASE TEMPLATE:

HOTEL FEASIBILITY STUDY PRESS RELEASE TEMPLATE

Firm Confirms Hotel is Feasible in COMMUNITY, STATE - DATE - Officials of COMMUNITY NAME in STATE were pleased to announce that the firm commissioned to complete a Hotel Market Feasibility Study for COMMUNITY, HOTEL FEASIBILITY STUDY COMPANY, is complete. The study indicated the greatest need in the area is in COMMUNITY, the POPULATION person community just AMOUNT minutes from NEAREST LARGE COMMUNITY, STATE.

"QUOTE FROM DRIVING PERSON IN THE COMMUNITY THAT DROVE THE HOTEL DEVELOPMENT IN REGARD TO WHAT PROCESS INTAILED, " said DRIVER'S NAME, DRIVER'S TITLE with DRIVER'S ORGANIZATION. " QUOTE FROM DRIVING PERSON IN THE COMMUNITY THAT INDICATES WHY THE ORGANIZATION CHOOSE THE PARTICULAR HOTEL FEASIBILITY COMPANY." The community took the initiative to make the investment in a Hotel Feasibility Study in SEASON of YEAR. In the coming months, COMMUNITY welcomed NAME OF CONSULTANT, a representative with NAME OF HOTEL FEASIBILITY COMPANY into their community for a tour and to sit down with local demand generators and community leaders.

"QUOTE FROM HOTEL FEASIBILITY CONSULTANT ABOUT OVERALL NEED," said NAME OF CONSULTANT, TITLE OF CONSULTANT of NAME OF HOTEL FEASIBILITY STUDY COMPANY. "QUOTE FROM HOTEL FEASIBILITY CONSULTANT ADDRESSING SPECIFIC AND LARGE DEMAND GENERATORS IN THE AREA." The Hotel Market Feasibility Study completed by HOTEL FEASIBILITY STUDY COMPANY in MONTH of YEAR indicated a need for SCALE lodging with NUMBER OF ROOMS RECOMMENDED rooms. They also indicated the property should offer amenities like LIST MAIN AMENITIES SUGGESTED BY THE HOTEL FEASIBILITY STUDY.

IF APPLICABLE - In addition, the research conducted by HOTEL FEASIBILITY STUDY COMPANY indicated a potential need for additional RETAIL/RESTAURANTS/FAMILY ENTERTAINMENT (whatever is identified in the study).
About HOTEL FEASIBILITY STUDY COMPANY NAME –
About COMMUNITY NAME -

Now that you have your template, who do you send it to? First, ensure you have permission to share. If you have not paid your full balance on the study, you do not own it yet. You will need to ensure you have all rights to the study before sharing. Here is a list of organizations you should get the completed press release to as soon as you receive the completed study, and have permission to share:

1. LOCAL AND REGIONAL CHAMBER OF COMMERCE - The Chambers in your area have a wonderful network of business owners that may be interested in being involved in the project. This could be as a landowner, as an investor, as a contractor, or may just know someone who may want to be interested.

2. LOCAL AND REGIONAL ECONOMIC DEVELOPMENT ORGANIZATIONS - Getting the word out to the Economic Development Organizations in the area can do the same thing as your Chamber of Commerce but it also may get them involved in potential incentive packages. I will go more in-depth when it comes to incentive packages in a later chapter as well.

3. LOCAL AND REGIONAL VISITORS BUREAUS - The Visitors Bureaus in your area, for a start should be overly excited about the idea of a new hotel coming. Their websites get a good amount of traffic. They will provide added excitement to the project and the more hype; the faster things will come together.

4. LOCAL TOURIST ATTRACTIONS - Tourist attractions, much like Visitors Bureaus have a large following. To top it off, most people on their mailing lists like to travel so giving them a heads up that there may be a hotel coming to town is a bonus!

5. LOCAL AND REGIONAL NEWSPAPERS - If you still have a newspaper, get them to put your press release in the paper as well as on their website. If they have an e-blast or newsletter, have them add the press release. Make sure it gets to as many people in the area as possible.

6. LOCAL AND REGIONAL TELEVISION STATIONS - Even if it is in a larger community, 30 miles or more away get the press release to them and push them to do a story on it. It should not be difficult in smaller communities. It can be a bit

difficult if you are a small community in the broadcast area of a larger community. Do not give up! Keep on them to do a story about the potential project. Be annoying!

7. LOCAL AND REGIONAL RADIO STATIONS - Believe it or not, radio is still a wonderful outlet to get the word out. Keep in mind that unlike televisions, you cannot fast forward through a radio commercial. Get the press release to as many radio stations that you can!

8. REGIONAL AND STATE GOVERNMENT ORGANIZATIONS - Obviously, you and whatever organization you work for (you know the ones that paid for the study and maybe even this book) know about your study but some do not. I once was working with a Chamber of Commerce that paid for a study. They did not want the people at City Hall to even know I was working in town to do a Comprehensive Hotel Market Feasibility Study. Strange. Get the word out to your fellow, local, and regional community leaders.

One thing to keep in mind, be prepared to have a lot of people reaching out to you that may be full of crud! In later chapters, we will go through vetting these people but always ensure you have your contact information in each release. Here is a checklist to help you through the process:

- o I sent my PR to the Chamber of Commerce.
- o I sent my PR to the Economic Development Corporation.
- o I sent my PR to the Local and Regional Visitors Bureaus.
- o I sent my PR to the Local and Regional Newspapers.
- o I sent my PR to the Local and Regional Television Stations.
- o I sent my PR to the Local and Regional Radio Stations.
- o I sent my PR to all additional organizations I feel would get the word out.

Chapter Seven

FINDING THE RIGHT HOTEL DEVELOPER

FINDING THE RIGHT HOTEL DEVELOPER

Hotel Developers are a dime a dozen! I am not being a smart mouth or sassy. It is true. As a person that has seen every aspect of the Hotel Development process, I have run into them all!

The developer that says they have investors in their pocket that will put their money in if you exclusively work with them. The developer that ties up the land for years and is never able to find an investor. The developer that has had twenty investor meetings, drummed up interest and has strung said investors along so long they have lost interest or just lost faith. I have seen it all!

Guess what happens when a developer gets involved that is not trustworthy?

Your project stalls, loses any momentum, and eventually, the study you have invested in is pointless. Your study's validity is only strong for two years. Any time after that and you are up a creek without a paddle. At one year you can pay for an update. This is typically half the cost of the original study but once you hit two years, it is a full redo. If anyone does finally decide to get the ball rolling after two years, you will need to purchase a new Comprehensive Hotel Feasibility Study.

Another thing to keep in mind is that other pieces of the hotel development puzzle can offer hotel development services. Many hotel management companies, hotel general contractors, and so on can offer these services. hotel brands/franchises cannot. Hotel franchises are strictly regulated against financial representation. You will learn more about this in another chapter, but it is important to understand the difference between a hotel franchise salesperson and a hotel developer. Hotel developers can promise you the sun and stars when it comes to revenue. A hotel franchise salesperson should not and legally cannot promise you ANYTHING!

Keep in mind, I have some experience as a hotel developer. I am not bashing the profession. Just like many other professions, there are some bad eggs but not all are bad. Let us get to how to find a hotel developer that is the right fit.

Vetting is an important part of the process. If a hotel developer is knocking on your door, you are not their first call. They have been up and down the highway seeking out communities that may have need. There is nothing wrong with that! When talking to or vetting a hotel developer, take these steps:

1. COLLEAGUES - As stated above, you are not the first door they are knocking on so talk to your sister communities down the road. See if they have heard from the developer/s. Ask them about their experience. A simple Google search of the person's name can give you a bit of information about projects they have worked on. Have they completed these projects? Talk to the officials of that community and find out if they would work with that person again.

2. REFERENCES - Always ask for references! I understand most people would not give people that had a poor experience, but you can get an understanding of how they work, their weaknesses, and their strengths. An additional way to uncover references, not on the developer's list, is to the references list if they know of

any other projects said developer worked on. You might just find a potential reference that was not given on the developer's list.

3. RESEARCH - As stated number 1, doing your research can uncover things that could be great and could be negative. Simply searching for a developer's company name will uncover past lawsuits or simply online complaints. I am not saying that you should take this information as fact but finding the information and reaching out to your colleague in that community may help you with your decision-making process.

4. KEEP OPEN - I hear the same story at least once a month. A community reaches out to me and asks for help because they put all their eggs in one basket. They have been working with a hotel developer for a year, two, or even more and nothing is happening. Or worse, they have not heard from said developer in months. Do not do this to yourself. The first one to get it done, wins! Keep your community open to development. Do not box yourself in by putting all your faith in one person too early in the process.

5. KNOWING WHEN TO COMMIT - When it comes to number 4, you also need to know when to commit to a developer. Once your hotel developer has an investor/s, land, financing, and a brand secured, this is the home stretch. Commit. If you do not, they could take their project to another community. They have gone the distance and it is time to get someone on paper. Do not let a competitor come in and make promises they cannot keep in the fourth quarter. I have worked with many communities that allow this to happen and it is detrimental.

I know of one hotel developer that works his butt off. He is the most organized and diligent hotel developer I have ever worked with. Three times, yes, I said three, community leaders (the city administrator and mayor) have pushed him out to work with someone else. His willingness to spend time on the project after the first time they decided someone was better baffles me.

This developer has come to the rescue many times and it is shameful how the city's officials have cast him aside to look at the shiny new hotel developer that is promising things he cannot do. Have some loyalty to the people that have been helping you and working hard to make your dreams of a new hotel possible. Rant over!

Following these steps will help ensure your project gets completed by someone you are comfortable with.

In some cases, a development agreement is put into place. These can be requested by your hotel developer or the community leaders. There are a few things you should ensure the developer agreement touches on:

1. COMMITMENTS OF EACH PARTY - I have reviewed extremely one-sided development agreements. Ensure your agreement is balanced and each party is getting their fair share.

Typical conditions include but are not limited to:

Utility Conditions
Zoning Conditions
Geotechnical Conditions
Building Permit Conditions
Site Permit Conditions
Signage Conditions
Easement, Covenants Restriction Conditions

Financing Conditions

Plan Approval Conditions

Flood Plain Conditions

Environmental Conditions

Waiver Conditions

Timeline Conditions

Quality Conditions

To help you with this process, I have made a simple checklist to follow:

- o I have reached out to my colleagues to ask about their experience.
- o I have reached out to references provided to ask about their experience.
- o I have done my research on each developer.
- o I have been open to new partnerships throughout the process.
- o I have addressed any potential incentives for a developer.
- o I have addressed any concerns with potential investors with the developer.
- o I have addressed any concerns with the potential financing for the developer.

- o I have addressed any concerns from the hotel brand about the developer.
- o I have drafted a developer agreement with the developer of choice.

Chapter Eight

FINDING THE RIGHT
INVESTOR/S

FINDING THE RIGHT INVESTOR/S

After you have the study and send out your press release, as stated before, you may people contacting you that are interested. You will have people coming out of the woodwork to offer their "services". If I say it once, I will say in a million times, do not buy into any hype until a deal is signed.

This book is all about not just finding investors but finding the right investors. For a hotel to succeed, you must have the right people involved in it.

When you are looking at putting together your group of investors, there are a few things to consider. The first thing to learn is there are a few types of investors:

1. REITS - This stands for Real Estate Investment Fund. These funds are run by large companies and large groups of investors. They typically own large portfolios of hotels. If you are in a sub-tertiary market or smaller, you will not get seen by these funds. You can reach for this star, but I am going to give it to you straight. Do not

waste your time unless you are in oil country or a large market.

2. LOCAL BUSINESS OWNERS - If you are in a sub-tertiary market or smaller, these potential investors will be your best bet. These are the hardware store owner, largest landowners, convenience store owner, large farmer, the family that sold their small canning company to a big company, and so on. These are the people in your community that are contributing the most to the economic development of your community. Talk to them! Send them the Comprehensive Hotel Market Feasibility Study IMMEDIATELY! Invite them to an investor meeting.

Extra Tip - Hopefully, you are reading this book before or while your study is being done. If you are, work on these investors during the process as well.

3. HOTEL DEVELOPERS - In many cases, the Hotel Developer will invest a small percentage into the project. This percentage is typically a portion of their fee. Just an FYI, Hotel Developers typically will take a fee of 3 to 5 percent of the project (3 for larger projects and 5 for smaller projects). You learned more about

what a Hotel Developer brings to the project in a previous chapter. If you have Hotel Developers in your area, reach out to them. If you wish to reach out on more of a national basis, feel free but you may not get a response in a small market.

4. HOTEL OWNERS - There is always a possibility that a current hotel owner in your community wants to invest in the project. If you have a current hotel owner in your community, make sure you get them the study. Do not get me wrong, they may be irritated by the fact that the hotel study was conducted but if I were in your shoes, I would remind said hotel owner of the reasoning behind the study being commissioned. Their hotel is too old. Their hotel is not clean. There are many reasons and a good hotel feasibility study will highlight them. The best way for the current Hotel Owner to capitalize on the new, shiny hotel is to be a part of it. Offer these people first dibs on being a part of the project.

Extra Tip - If management is an issue, you may want to simply ask for the hotel owner to be a part of the investment. In some cases, hotel brands are picky about who can manage their hotels. A professional management company may be your best bet.

5. HOTEL MANAGEMENT COMPANIES - There are many hotel management companies out there looking for opportunities. You may be able to pique their interest. If you have a hotel management company in your local area reach out to them.

6. LANDOWNERS - You know the person or families in town that own most of the commercial land or land in general in your community? Their land was most likely on the list of potential sites for your Comprehensive Hotel Feasibility Study. Send them the study and see if they are interested in, at the minimum investing their land. Remember to keep strong! There are certain types of people in the landowner biz that like to hike up the price of land because a "hotel" is coming to town. Keep in mind that there are many other land opportunities and if this happens, be prepared to walk away, and move on to the next landowner.

P.S. I say "YOUR" because this is YOUR process. Whether you lead and let others do the work or pull the group together, this is YOUR project.

When you are talking to potential investors about our hotel project, do me a favor and let the Comprehensive Hotel Feasibility Study speak for the project. The key is to know the study is accurate and then to understand it. Here are a few steps to take before you pitch to those investors:

1. READ THE STUDY - This may seem crazy but there are so many people in your position that do not read the study they purchased. They may check through it for errors, but they do not read it to gain an understanding of why the firm hired, came to their determination. Take your knowledge of the area out of the situation. Read it as though you are a person looking to invest in a project. Read it as though you are a person that knows nothing about your community. Based on the information provided, would you invest? Now ask yourself if it is true.

2. UNDERSTAND THE FINANCIAL PROFORMA - You may not be a banker and you may not be the person investing but you will need to answer simple questions about the financials. It could be as simple as understanding how the returns were configured or it could be as complicated as understanding what each

line item means. The point is, if you do not do anything else to help your project, know the proforma front and back. Take the time to get on the phone with the firm hired and go through that thing line by line. Make sure there are zero errors before you give it to investors. Even if it is a small error, it can hurt the credibility of what you are trying to do.

3. ONGOING INVESTOR RELATIONS - This is a given for you. You will need to hold hands. You know this and you are used to it. You do not need to understand this, the firm you hired to conduct your Comprehensive Hotel Feasibility Study does. They need to answer a question from investors or potential investors until this project is complete. Make sure they have a firm grasp of this before even picking them. Once the study is complete, remind them of it. There will be plenty of people throughout the process there to help them but the company that did the first report should be available to help them understand it. As mentioned before, make sure this service is included in the cost listed in the agreement.

Now that you have yourself set-up for investor pitching and relations success, you need to know how to identify the right investors. There is no real "perfect investor" for a hotel. Investors in hotels can be anyone.

The key is to find the perfect investor is finding the right investor for your community. The investors that are in it to make money but also care about how this development will impact your community.

I met a man once that was a remarkably successful hotel investor. His company had hotels across the county that they had invested in. As I spoke to him, we determined that he had owned two large full-service hotels in the area I live in. I knew they had gone back to the bank, but I did not want to bring it up. Little did I know, he was proud of the fact that they went back to the bank. He brought it up. He had a non-recourse loan with little down (pre-recession). His company took the money out of the hotel, each month. When the economy crashed, they handed the keys back to the bank. No harm, no foul in his mind. What would happen if this happened to your new hotel in your community? Would it be bought right away? Maintained by the bank? Would it sit empty for 3 years while the bank tried their best to sell it with no avail? Meanwhile, the pipes are busting, and the bank cannot afford to update the property or just does not want to put any more money into it? Will it be purchased by someone that will run it into the ground?

I promise you this, once the hotel is built you do not have much control over what happens to it. Honestly, unless you are investing your money, you do not have much control over what happens to the hotel project now and moving forward. What you do have control over is the type of investors/people that are involved in the project.

Do your research. Ask for references. Do not ask for three, as for all of them! Ask around about the person that is interested in investing in your hotel project. If you live in a small town, you probably already know them. Ask the investor what their intentions are in the project. Are they looking to build it and get out in a year or ten? There is no correct answer to these questions. You just need to understand the intentions of the investor. Their intentions not being in line with what you want is not necessarily a bad thing. Their intentions not being in line with the other investors you have spoken to may be an obstacle. Make sure everyone is on the same page.

Pitching the opportunity is key so have an investor meeting. Have a party!? Maybe. Whatever works in your situation? Call a meeting to ensure everyone is on the same page. Go over questions our potential investors may have and if needed, bring in the hotel feasibility study firm you hired. It can simply be on a conference call (your firm will charge you to come back for additional visits). The point is getting everything on the table and be clear and concise. The next page offers a good example of a Prospective Hotel Investor Introduction Meeting Agenda.

POTENTIAL HOTEL INVESTOR MEETING AGENDAY

DATE - TIME - PLACE

AGENDA

Hotel Feasiblity Study Discussion
1. Review Market Demand Generators
2. Review Projected Hotel Constuction Costs
3. Review Projected Hotel Proforma
Questions about Hotel Feasibility Study

Investment Structure
Introduction of Hotel Developer (THIS SHOULD BE IN
PLACE AND THEY SHOULD RUN THIS PORTION OF THE
MEETING)
TOTAL AMOUNT NEEDED
MINIMUM INVESTMENT REQUIRED
INTENTIONAL FINANCING STRUCTURE
EXPECTED BRAND
EXPECTED MANAGEMENT COMPANY

Call for investment

PLEASE CONTACT
NAME
COMPANY NAME
POSITION
PHONE
EMAIL
COMPANY WEBSITE
FOR MORE INFORMATION
ABOUT THIS OPPORTUNITY.

Reminder, you can also download this and all the other templates in this book at

www.theultimatehoteldevelopmentguide.com !

Utilize this checklist through the process of uncovering your investors:

Investor Types

- o I have reached out to potential real estate investment funds that may want to participate.
- o I have reached out to local business owners and landowners that may want to participate.
- o I have reached out to hotel developers that may want to participate.
- o I have reached out to local and regional hotel owners that may want to participate.
- o I have reached out to local and regional hotel management companies that may want to participate.

Investor Meeting

- o I have compiled a list of potential investors for the project.
- o I have a strong understanding of the hotel study and its recommendations.
- o I have a strong understanding of the financial proforma in the study.
- o I have contacted all potential investors to schedule an investor meeting.
- o I have scheduled the investor meeting.
- o I have completed the agenda and sent it to all potential investors.

Chapter Nine

FINDING THE RIGHT FINANCING

FINDING THE RIGHT FINANCING

There are three things you can work on while the Hotel Feasibility Study is being complete to ensure your project does not stall:

1. Find Investors

2. Find Financing

3. Find Land

If you have good prospects for each of these in hand when you receive the final draft of the hotel feasibility study, the other things come into place a lot faster. There are chapters on each. This chapter is focused on how to find the right Hotel Financing for your project. If you are already working with a Hotel Developer, they may already have something in mind but always know that if for some reason that person disappears, you should have as much information as possible to keep the project on the right path.

Finding financing can be difficult in some communities and easy in others. The point is to understand your hurdles as soon as possible. Talk to the financial institutions in your community right away! Find out these things immediately:

1. INTEREST - Not the interest rate but the financial institution's actual interest in the project. Some will not even want to be a party to it. Find that out right away. Do not waste your time.

3. CAPABILITY - You should have an idea of how much your project will cost. Find out what their lending limits are. Find out what type of equity they would like to see in a loan the size of the project. Do they work with SBA Loans? Do they work with USDA Loans?

2. INDUSTRY - Certain financial institutions can only offer so much financing to hotels or simply the hospitality industry. Find out if they are even in the position to lend monies for a hotel.

Once you have determined these things, start to dig into what they may be willing to offer (I say "may" because you do not have a study yet). Organize this information with the worksheet, HOTEL FINANCING WORKSHEET on the following page.

THIS WORKSHEET WILL HELP YOU THROUGH THE PROCESS OF FINDING THE RIGHT HOTEL FINANCING FOR YOUR PROJECT.

FINANCING OPTIONS

OPTION ONE	OPTION TWO	OPTION THREE	OPTION FOUR
Name	Name	Name	Name
Willing/Capable	Willing/Capable	Willing/Capable	Willing/Capable
Interest	Interest	Interest	Interest
Equity Required	Equity Required	Equity Required	Equity Required
Financing Type	Financing Type	Financing Type	Financing Type

FINANCING INSTITUTION CHOSEN

NAME OF INSTITUTION	
NAME OF CONTACT	
EMAIL/PHONE	

Reminder, you can also download this and all the other templates in this book at

www.theultimatehoteldevelopmentguide.com !

Now that you have all the information gathered, verified, and ready to go, give it to your chosen hotel developer. If for some reason you are not working with a hotel developer, give it to the hotel investor/s that will be putting the project together. This information can also be given in the RFP you send out to attract hotel developers, hotel investors, hotel brands, and hotel management companies. The key is that you have helped the process along making it more efficient for the company that decides to move forward with the project.

Another piece of information to keep in mind is if you do go with a hotel developer, by finding interested financial institutions, you have taken care of a task they are paid to do. Keep in mind that although you have done this leg work, there are a lot of pieces in the financing aspect of your project that still need to be done. The paperwork alone is daunting. With all this in the back of your head, having the financing due diligence done is helpful and will help you attract a hotel developer faster. If you decided to try and get a fee reduction, you may be out of luck. There is much more to be done and they may or may not budge.

Chapter Eleven

FINDING THE RIGHT
BRAND

FINDING THE RIGHT BRAND

Depending on how you originally started the process, you may have already spoken to a hotel franchise developer. They may have even been the person that suggested getting a Comprehensive Hotel Feasibility Study. One thing to know is that when a person is selling franchises (as a side note, I have sold a few franchises so I am well versed), they are not allowed to discuss returns or how the hotel may do. When I say, "not allowed", I mean it is a crime. Therefore, in most cases, they recommend getting a Hotel Feasibility Study.

Hotel brands are awesome! they provide the hotel with so many great things like recognition, marketing, consistently, training, and so on. The key is to have the right brand for the price, market, and scale needed in the community. Let us address each of them:

1. PRICE - Upfront and ongoing pricing are particularly important when looking at hotel brands. For instance, if you are in a town of 2500 people and your Hotel Feasibility Study recommends a 40 room, upper mid-scale hotel, you may not want to call Hilton. Besides the

fact that they will most definitely, not return your call, the fees involved may not be a good fit. Let us take Hampton Inn & Suites by Hilton. Great brand! There is not much you can say in the negative column when it comes to a Hampton Inn & Suites. The thing is, in some markets, you may do just as well if you are a Comfort Inn and the initial and ongoing price tag may be extremely different. Between the ongoing Franchise Fees and the products that you are required to buy through required vendors, most certainly at an up-charge, operating a Hampton Inn & Suites can cost up to 17% off the top more. This could be up to 40% of your net profit. In many markets, the amount of business the Hilton brings you is well worth it. I would bet their Franchisee Satisfaction Rating is one of the highest, but you must know where to locate them.

2. MARKET - There are some markets that you will need to go with a larger brand and some that it is not needed. Like I mentioned earlier, in some cases, you will not even get a call back from a Hotel Franchise Developer. I have worked with communities I thought would easily support a Residence Inn by Marriott, but the community's leaders would never get a return phone call. Some brands require certain things around

a hotel. Some brands require more than 80 rooms. Some brands require a certain population count. Some brands require an investor to buy multiple Hotel Franchises vs. just one. There are many reasons to search around and get a better understanding of what may be a good fit for your specific community.

3. SCALE - There are many different scales in the hotel industry and unfortunately it is not very cost-effective to build an economy hotel these days. Besides the cost of constructing a hotel going up over 40% in some cases, the customer will only pay so much to stay at a Days Inn. I do not care how nice it is! The consumer has it in their head that, unless it is a special event, they will only pay so much for an economy hotel. Your study should give you a recommendation of what scale the demand in your community is leaving for. Use that to start seeking out the right Hotel Brand for your community.

Use our HOTEL BRAND WORKSHEET below to look at the potential brands that could be a good fit for your community and have the research in hand when speaking with potential Hotel Investors and Hotel Developers.

SCALE/CHAIN OPTIONS

NUMBER OF ROOMS RECOMMENDED BY YOUR HOTEL MARKET FEASIBILITY STUDY

BRANDS RECOMMENDED BY YOUR HOTEL MARKET FEASIBILITY STUDY

SPECIFIC AMENITIES RECOMMENDED BY YOUR HOTEL MARKET FEASIBILITY STUDY

RATE RANGE RECOMMENDED BY YOUR HOTEL MARKET FEASIBILITY STUDY

BRANDING PARTNERS THAT HAVE ALREADY SHOWN INTEREST

Brand 1

Brand 2

Brand 3

Brand 4

Brand 5

Notes:

Option One

Name ▊▊▊▊▊▊▊▊▊▊▊▊▊

All-in Per Room Cost
of Construction ▊▊▊▊▊▊

Upfront/Initial Fees ▊▊▊▊▊▊

Ongoing
Franchise/Royalty Fees ▊▊▊▊▊▊

Ongoing Loyalty
Program Fees ▊▊▊▊▊▊

Ongoing
Technology Fees ▊▊▊▊▊▊

Ongoing Third-Party
Internet Booking Fees ▊▊▊▊▊▊

Expected Brand
Contribution ▊▊▊▊▊▊

Closest Hotel Under
Same Name ▊▊▊▊▊▊

Option Two

Name ▊▊▊▊▊▊▊▊▊▊▊▊▊

All-in Per Room Cost
of Construction ▊▊▊▊▊▊

Upfront/Initial Fees ▊▊▊▊▊▊

Ongoing
Franchise/Royalty Fees ▊▊▊▊▊▊

Ongoing Loyalty
Program Fees ▊▊▊▊▊▊

Ongoing
Technology Fees ▊▊▊▊▊▊

Ongoing Third-Party
Internet Booking Fees ▊▊▊▊▊▊

Expected Brand
Contribution ▊▊▊▊▊▊

Closest Hotel Under
Same Name ▊▊▊▊▊▊

WHICH OF THE TWO BRANDING OPTIONS MAKE THE BEST BUSINESS SENSE FOR YOUR COMMUNITY?

BRANDING CHOSEN

NAME OF
INSTITUTION ▊▊▊▊▊▊▊▊▊▊▊▊▊

NAME OF
CONTACT ▊▊▊▊▊▊▊▊▊▊▊▊▊

EMAIL/PHONE ▊▊▊▊▊▊▊▊▊▊▊▊▊

Notes:

Chapter Twelve

FINDING THE RIGHT MANAGEMENT COMPANY

FINDING THE RIGHT MANAGEMENT COMPANY

When I was a Vice President of Development for a Hotel Brand a few years back, I had a client that I sold a franchise to. He was a lawyer that built the hotel years ago, had bought out all his other investors, had paid the hotel off, and essentially thought of the property as a retirement fund. He did not have a Hotel Management Company. The hotel owner had hired a Hotel General Manager (GM) that he trusted completely.

This GM had brought him from barely making money each year to running a smooth and profitable hotel. When I went to the hotel for the first time, I had a gut feeling that something was off. The GM was not as forthcoming about the operations of the hotel as I would have liked. As someone that has extensive experience in the day-to-day operations of a hotel, I saw things that bugged me. I brought them up and simply suggested the owner hire a professional management company, but he trusted his manager and I was new to his world. I did not have his trust like his manager did. Throughout the next two years, I worked with him to do the best I could to be the person he could come to with issues. The person that could and would willingly help with solutions.

It was about two years after he signed the franchise agreement with my company that he called me upset. He had been a bit suspicious, so he started to look a little closer at the books. During that call, he informed me that he believed the manager had embezzled more than $90,000 from the hotel in that year alone. He was in the process of hiring a forensic accountant to investigate it more and was devastated. It seemed that the manager had been taking many cash-paying guests into the hotel and the cash from those rooms went right into that manager's pocket. This was just what he was certain of at the time. He would have to look at all the years that person worked for him costing him even more money and time.

If this hotel owner would have had a management company, it would have cost him around $50,000 per year. This cost seems like a lot but in the grand scheme of things is a drop in the bucket of what a hotel owner/investor can lose if someone with a trained eye is not looking at the hotel and its operations daily. Not to mention the peace of mind it should bring.

Although there is a good amount of Hotel Management Companies out there, they are not alike. Their pricing ranges substantially. The way they report and operate can be are completely different as well. Some will not even look at a hotel that is less than 100 rooms or a certain brand.

I know this because I had a client that was in search for a Hotel Management Company at one time. They asked me to do some due diligence and send them some proposals. I was happy to help. I reached out to nearly 20 different contacts I had at the largest Hotel Management Companies in the United States. Luckily, my contacts were nice enough to at least give it to me straight. Responses like "that is too small" or "it is not worth our time" were common. Luckily, my business partner and I have over fifty years of experience in Hotel Management and decided to take on the hotel ourselves. The point is that you must find the right Hotel Management Company and there are a few things you need to keep an eye out for when doing so:

1. PRICING - I have seen many of our competitors put in their Hotel Feasibility Studies that the rate for Hotel Management Services is 3%. Each time I see this I roll my eyes. Do not get me wrong, there are plenty of hotels paying this percentage, but they are not your typical hotels. Hotels paying 3% are large hotels. They are in top markets and grossing millions and millions of dollars. I offer a service to my clients where I review hotel management and franchise agreements. Most management contracts or agreements I review are in the range of 5% and 6% of Gross Profit. Not to mention the upfront costs and costs during construction.

2. EXPERIENCE - This is important. I say this from a person that owns part of a Hotel Management Company, that has sought out a management company for clients and as a person that has worked for some of the largest and smallest in the country. Look at the principal people in the company you are looking at and their experience in the industry. Do they have experience with new-build hotels? Even if they do not, have they ever worked for a company that did and went through the process? Another aspect of the company's experience is in some cases, the brand chosen must approve the management company. You will need to

keep this in mind when looking into the companies you are vetting.

3. ELBOW GREASE - This one is big for me. There is nothing worse than a company that is happy to take the upfront and monthly fees but will not do the work. Ask the companies you are looking into about the attention and man-hours they expect both on-property and at their corporate office in the first year. Ask them how often a person from the company will be at the hotel to check on things. Ask to see a sample of the Profit and Loss Statements they provide investors each month. Ask them for references from other investors groups they work for currently. Ask them how much training they provide. Get a good understanding of how much elbow grease they will be putting forth in your project.

The Hotel Management Company you work with is crucial to the success of your property. Utilize this HOTEL MANAGEMENT WORKSHEET to ensure you have covered all your bases:

MANAGEMENT COMPANY OPTIONS

Option One

Name	
Years of Experience	
Brand Approved	
Term of Contract	
Upfront Management Fee	
Ongoing Management Fee	

Option Two

Name	
Years of Experience	
Brand Approved	
Term of Contract	
Upfront Management Fee	
Ongoing Management Fee	

WHICH OF THE TWO MANAGEMENT COMPANY OPTIONS MAKE THE BEST BUSINESS SENSE FOR YOUR COMMUNITY?

NAME OF INSTITUTION	
NAME OF CONTACT	
EMAIL/PHONE	

Chapter Thirteen

UTILIZING A HOTEL DEVELOPMENT RFP

UTILIZING A HOTEL DEVELOPMENT RFP

There are many instances where a Request for Proposal may be in the best way to attract a NEW HOTEL to your community. There are also instances where it is not a great idea. I have seen RFPs come out throughout my career that simply made me think the potential client was high-maintenance and made me not want to help them with their project. I have even reviewed Hotel Development RFPs that exposed the person creating it as a not educated on what the RFP should look like. When you look at those situations, they can even be a deterrent to simply responding. You do not want that at all! Let us address both. Then you can decide what is right for you and your community.

WHAT NOT TO DO

Let us get the negative out of the way.

As stated above, I have read hundreds of REQUESTS FOR PROPOSALS. I would say that 90 percent of them have requests, descriptions of tasks, information, and so on that are not necessary and will turn companies off from the project. I am telling you, hotel brands, developers, management companies, construction companies are all remarkably busy and do not need your business right now. They will work for your business, but they will not do more work than they feel is needed. If you add things to your scope of work that are not necessary to the project, you will lose a percentage of your responses. Having a good understanding of what is needed is a great place to start so make sure that you educated yourself (much like reading this book).

Here are a few mistakes community leaders make when creating their RFP for a NEW HOTEL DEVELOPMENT in their town:

LACK OF KNOWLEDGE - Like stated above, you need to educate yourself on the process. Do not just read an article on a hotel that is being developed and think you are going to write a fruitful RFP for a NEW HOTEL DEVELOPMENT. You have already taken the first step by reading this book, so you get an "A".

ASKING TOO MUCH - Do not get me wrong, some companies have money to waste on your pointless requests or demands but most do not unless they are making money on a project. Short of time, printing costs for the proposal response, shipping cost, and maybe a flash drive with the proposal on it, you should not request anything additional besides information. I have had RFPs that required a hotel rendering. Do you know how much a hotel rendering costs? I have seen renderings run over $8,000. Why would a hotel developer spend that sort of money to respond to someone asking for their help? I understand they stand to gain much more money than that if the project comes to light, but that sort of investment is a gamble that most will not take. Be reasonable in your request.

NOT SHOWING BENEFIT - I have reviewed many hotel development RFPs that are extremely imbalanced. You need to show the benefits to the company reviewing the RFP to work with you and your community. A good partnership is built on both parties benefiting from the project.

NOT HAVING A CONVERSATION - I cannot tell you how many times I have tried to speak with the person that sent me the RFP to no avail. They did not want to speak with me. They wanted their proposal and that was it. No conversation to, at the minimum, gain an understanding of the person responding's personality, their approach, or what the company responding is all about. Invite conversations throughout the process. You will have a much better understanding of the people you will be dealing with and possibly even prevent personality clashes while working on the project.

OUTSOURCING - My blood boils when I get an RFP from a third-party company. These companies get paid thousands, if not tens of thousands of dollars to send a boilerplate template with no real personal touch and no real knowledge of the community. That is no good and will hurt you and the future of your project. Do not spend this money on something that you can do yourself.

WHAT TO DO

I can tell you that when I get an RFP I am always on the fence on if I like this method or not. This is mainly due to the lack of preparation on the part of the preparer. Let us talk about some things that you should include in your RFP.

TIMELINE - When it comes to hotel development, timelines can be hard to keep but that does not mean you cannot set them. If you give a person a goal, they are more likely to achieve that goal than if you have no goal. Put a goal in place but make sure you are reasonable in your goal. It takes more than a few months to complete a hotel development project.

QUALITY NOT QUANTITY - When you are asking companies to first spend their time to submit a proposal to you, no matter how extensive, make sure you are asking for things that are important to the project. I once had an RFP ask for information on each person in our company. Not just the people that would potentially be working on the project but EVERYONE! That is just intrusive and, dare I say, a bit rude. I am not going to give you the resume of the person getting my lunch. Their position/role has nothing to do with the project and you do not have a right to the information. Do not be that person. Ask for pertinent information and you will get what you need without question.

REFERENCES - ASK FOR THEM! I am sure you have noticed throughout this book; I am big on references. I feel it is a complete disservice to your project if you do not get an extensive list of references. I can TELL you all sorts of crazy things about myself and my company. You will get the truth from references so ask them! I know some people think references given by a potential service provider only have positive experiences to talk about, but that is not true! I have people on my reference list that I know we messed up a thing or two, but we are also proud of how we address our missteps. Ask the questions you need to ask and do not be shy! My company gives out all of our client's information. I am sure that some had mixed opinions on certain topics but I KNOW that they will all say we took care of them and did not back away from a challenge, even if we created that challenge for ourselves.

DIY - A big one for me is to D.I.Y. As mentioned in the last section, I am not a fan of hiring people to do things that I am capable of. Especially when there are much more economical options out there that will let me take control of my outcome.

Chapter Fourteen

HOW TO COMPOSE YOUR HOTEL DEVELOPMENT REQUEST FOR PROPOSAL

HOW TO COMPOSE YOUR HOTEL DEVELOPMENT REQUEST FOR PROPOSAL

WHAT YOU WILL NEED

Photos - Highlight the beauty of your community as well as any other things that can attract the companies looking at your request for proposal. Ensure these photos are of high quality. Follow this checklist when you are reviewing the photos chosen to highlight your community:

01 DOES MY RFP OFFER AT LEAST 5 PHOTOS OF MY COMMUNITY?

02 ARE THE PHOTOS IN MY RFP OF HIGH QUALITY IN BOTH DIGITAL AND PRINT FORM?

03 HAVE I HIGHLIGHTED AT LEAST TWO TOURISM ATTRACTIONS?

04 HAVE I HIGHLIGHTED AT LEAST ONE BUSINESS DEMAND GENERATORS OR TOP EMPLOYERS?

05 HAVE I HIGHLIGHTED AT LEAST ONE OF OUR RECREATION DEMAND GENERATORS?

06 HAVE I INCLUDED AT LEAST ONE PHOTO THAT HIGHLIGHTS A HISTORIC OR A SCENIC ASPECT OF OUR COMMUNITY?

The people reviewing your RFP, in most cases, have not been to your community so it is best to ensure your photos help them understand why they should respond to your RFP.

COMMUNITY PROFILE - Your community profile is important. I know you have paid for and included a hotel feasibility study, but I would bet most people receiving your RFP do not review it thoroughly, if at all. Ensure each of the following sections are clear, concise, and get them hooked.

CURRENT ECONOMIC PROFILE - This section will be a more extensive description of the community. Highlight the top employers and any growth/expansion they have had recently.

COMMUNITY HIGHLIGHTS - This section should offer puller points on the community. They should be as follows:
1. Population
2. Median Household Income
3. Traffic Count
4. Unemployment Rate
5. Average Home Price

FUTURE ECONOMIC DEVELOPMENT PROFILE - This section will be focused on any future growth in the area that you can speak about. This can be businesses that are planning on expending in your community or companies that plan to move to your community.

COMMUNITY TOURISM PROFILE - This section will be focused on any tourism attractions in your area. If you have a museum, let the RFP participant know of the out of town travelers that visit each year. If you have a golf course, let them know about any large tournaments. Let them know what your community has to offer people traveling to or through your area.

COMMUNITY ECONOMIC INCENTIVE HIGHLIGHTS - You may want to make the font larger on this section (I am sort of kidding and sort of serious). The people looking at your RFP will most likely skip to this section before even glancing at the rest. They will want to know there is something in it for them. This is the case with many of the companies that you are sending this RFP to. If you are not offering any incentive, it may be beneficial to leave this part out but if you are, make sure it can be seen right away!

SITE/LAND SELECTION INFORMATION - Ensure this section offers detailed information about the site/sites selected in the hotel feasibility study. If there are any additional sites to be considered, please include them as well. Having multiple options is not a bad thing and one company may prefer a certain type of location for a site over another.

HOTEL FEASIBILITY STUDY HIGHLIGHTS - As stated above, most people will not truly read the actual hotel feasibility study so ensure you are offering a synopsis of the work. Make sure your sections offer a recap on the following:
-Demand Generator Summary
-Lodging Supply Summary
-Proposed Site Summary
-Economic Overview Summary
-Proposed Hotel Summary

Some of these things were already covered but you need to focus on what the hotel feasibility study states. There may be fewer sites in the study. The point of this section is the make it easy for the reader to breeze through the findings.

SELECTION TIMELINE/REQUIREMENTS/CRITERIA - PLEASE! PLEASE! Make sure you are clear in this section. Your timeline needs to be clear and offer a deadline. Make sure any contract you sign has a timeline and selection date in place. It is difficult to put a timeline on the building being complete. You can shoot for the completion of the first step or two. Once you have gathered all your investors and vendors, you may have a better shot at a completion date.

Now that you understand all the pieces you need to complete your HOTEL DEVELOPMENT RFP; you can get it started! The following pages give you a template to follow when laying your RFP out:

REQUEST FOR
PROPOSALS

HOTEL
DEVELOPMENT

THE COMMUNITY OF COMMUNITY NAME, STATE REQUESTS YOU PARTICIPATE IN THEIR HOTEL DEVELOPMENT PROCESS BY DEADLINE DATE

THE NAME OF ORGANIZATION IS SEEKING PROPOSALS FROM QUALIFIED HOTEL DEVELOPMENT, MANAGEMENT AND GENERAL CONTRACTOR FIRMS TO DEVELOP A SCALE HOTEL WITHIN THEIR COMMUNITY. THE CHOSEN COMPANY/COMPANIES MUST BE PROFICIENT IN COMMUNITY FACILITATION, POSITIVE ENGAGEMENT, AS WELL AS NOTED INDUSTRY EXPERIENCE AND KNOWLEDGE.

IF YOUR COMPANY WISHES TO BE CONSIDERED FOR THIS PROJECT, PLEASE EMAIL A COPY OF YOUR PROPOSAL TO NAME OF CONTACT AT EMAIL ADDRESS.

PHOTO HIGHLIGHTING COMMUNITY

THIS SECTION IS TO HIGHLIGHT
THE GREAT THINGS ABOUT YOUR
COMMUNITY IN REGARDS TO
TOURISM AND ECONOMIC GROWTH

CONTINUE
COMMUNITY
HIGHLIGHTS

PHOTO/S
HIGHLIGHTING
COMMUNITY

CONTINUE COMMUNITY
HIGHLIGHTS

WHAT YOU NEED TO KNOW ABOUT COMMUNITY NAME

ECONOMIC INCENTIVES AVAILABLE

THE NAME OF ORGANIZATION IS SEEKING PROPOSALS FROM QUALIFIED HOTEL DEVELOPMENT, MANAGEMENT AND GENERAL CONTRACTOR FIRMS TO DEVELOP A SCALE HOTEL WITHIN THEIR COMMUNITY. THE CHOSEN COMPANY/COMPANIES MUST BE PROFICIENT IN COMMUNITY FACILITATION, POSITIVE ENGAGEMENT, AS WELL AS NOTED INDUSTRY EXPERIENCE AND KNOWLEDGE.

PROPOSED SITE INFORMATION

WHAT YOU NEED TO KNOW ABOUT COMMUNITY NAME

HOTEL FEASIBILITY STUDY HIGHLIGHTS

THE NAME OF ORGANIZATION IS SEEKING PROPOSALS FROM QUALIFIED HOTEL DEVELOPMENT, MANAGEMENT AND GENERAL CONTRACTOR FIRMS TO DEVELOP A SCALE HOTEL WITHIN THEIR COMMUNITY. THE CHOSEN COMPANY/COMPANIES MUST BE PROFICIENT IN COMMUNITY FACILITATION, POSITIVE ENGAGEMENT, AS WELL AS NOTED INDUSTRY EXPERIENCE AND KNOWLEDGE.

DEMAND GENERATOR SUMMARY

LODGING SUPPLY SUMMARY

PROPOSED SITE/SITES SUMMARY

ECONOMIC OVERVIEW SUMMARY

PROPOSED HOTEL SUMMARY

SELECTION TIMELINE, REQUIREMENTS AND CRITERIA

SELECTION TIMELINE:

DATE   **PROPOSAL SUBMITTED**

DATE   **PHONE INTERVIEWS OF TOP THREE PROPOSALS**

DATE   **SELECT FIRM AND ISSUE CONTRACT**

PROJECT INFORMATION PROVIDED IN THIS RFP:

- HOTEL FEASIBILITY STUDY AND FINANCIAL PROJECTIONS CONDUCTED BY HOTEL FEASIBILITY STUDY COMPANY NAME
- COMMUNITY NAME TOURISM MARKETING COLLATERAL
- COMMUNITY NAME ECONOMIC DEVELOPMENT HIGHLIGHTS
- COMMUNITY NAME AREA ATTRACTION HIGHLIGHTS
- COMMUNITY NAME DEMAND GENERATOR HIGHLIGHTS
- COMMUNITY NAME ECONOMIC INCENTIVE HIGHLIGHTS

EACH PROPOSAL MUST, AT THE MINIMUM OFFER THE FOLLOWING:

- A LIST OF SIMILAR PROJECTS COMPLETED
- A LIST OF INDUSTRY RELATED REFERENCES INCLUDING NAME, TITLE, COMPANY, PROJECT DESCRIPTION, EMAIL AND PHONE NUMBER
- RESUMES OF PROFESSIONAL STAFF MEMBERS THAT WILL WORK ON THE PROJECT
- NAME OF PERSON TO BE IN CHARGE OF PROJECT
- A DESCRIPTION OF THE FIRM'S PROPOSED PROJECT APPROACH, DEMONSTRATING AN UNDERSTANDING OF THE PROJECT AND ITS INTENDED DELIVERABLES
- A DETAILED DESCRIPTION OF ESTIMATED COST FOR PROJECT INCLUDING CONSTRUCTION, FF&E, PRE-OPENING EXPENSES AND OTHER SOFT COSTS
- ESTIMATED PROJECT TIMELINE FROM EXECUTION OF PURCHSE AGREEMENT THROUGH OPENING
- DESIGNATED CONTACT PERSON WITH NAME, TITLE, PHONE AND EMAIL INFORMATION

THE COMPANY SELECTED WILL BE DONE SO BY THE FOLLOWING CRITERIA:

- EXPERIENCE, EXPERTISE AND CREDIBILITY OF THE COMPANY'S TEAM
- DEMONSTRATED SUCCESS BY THE COMPANY IN COMPLETING PROJECTS
- DIVERSITY IN FUNDING SOURCES
- PROPOSED SCHEDULE
- QUALITY AND PROFESSIONALISM OF SUBMITTED PROPOSAL
- CAPABILITIES TO PROVIDE REQUIRED SERVICES
- DEMONSTRABLE EXPERIENCE WORKING WITH SIMILAR SIZED COMMUNITIES
- PROJECT MANAGER EXPERIENCE AND QUALIFICATIONS
- STRENGTH AND EXPERIENCE OF ASSIGNED STAFF
- PROJECT UNDERSTANDING AND APPROACH
- REFERENCES

TOURS AND PRESENTATIONS

TOURS OF COMMUNITY AND SITE WILL BE SCHEDULED THROUGH THE LOCAL OFFICIALS BELOW:

THE COMMUNITY INTENDS TO SELECT ONE OR MORE RESPONDENTS TO MAKE IN-PERSON PRESENTATIONS TO THE SELECTION COMMITTEE BEFORE IDENTIFYING A TEAM WITH WHICH TO BEGIN NEGOTIATIONS FOR THE AGREEMENTS.

CONTACT INFORMATION

THIS SECTION WILL HAVE THE CONTACT INFORMATION OF PERSON VETTING THE RFPS

ATTACHED INFORMATION

THIS SECTION WILL THE LIST OF ATTACHMENTS TO YOUR RFP

THIS SECTION CAN BE FOR ADDITIONAL PHOTOS BUT WILL MOST LIKELY BE USED BY PREVIOUS SECTIONS.

You can also download this and all the other templates in this book at www.theultimatehoteldevelopmentguide.com !

WHO TO SEND YOUR RFP TO?

After you have your finished product, it can be a bit overwhelming to think about where you should send it. Here is a list of the types of companies you should be getting your hotel development RFP in front of. Keep in mind that you can simply Google these company types and build a list of contacts:

HOTEL DEVELOPERS - Hotel Developers will be one of the first steps in the Hotel Development process and can be your one-stop-shop for the entire process. They are the first piece of your puzzle.

HOTEL MANAGEMENT COMPANIES - Hotel Management Companies can also be Hotel Developers but in some cases, they simply manage the hotel. They also have contacts at Hotel Brands. Getting your project in front of a reputable Hotel Management Company can get you through many doors!

HOTEL BRANDS - If your RFP does not pique the interest of a Hotel Developer, it should a Hotel Brand. If your project interests a brand, they can help you get in contact with a Hotel Developer or Management

Company that may be interested. Having a Hotel Brand interested in your market can only get your project in front of people that are doing projects. A Hotel Brand cannot solicit investors, landowners, and so on due to the strong government restrictions on financial representation.

WHAT TO DO WITH THE RESPONSES

After your required deadline for submitting, you will need to go through the process of reviewing the responses. Use our HOTEL DEVELOPMENT RFP RESPONSE WORKSHEET to tally up the requirements. For each company, rate each category, 1 to 5 (5 being best) and total them up:

Name	
Company Experience	
Past Success	
Proposed Schedule	
Funding Sources	
Professionalism of Proposal	
Project Understanding	
Staff Experience	
Reference Quality	
Total	

Now that you have taken your responses and put them into the worksheet, you need to decide. If you have investors interested in the project, you will need them to review the responses. If you have a bank interested in the project, you will need to bring them in on the discussion. The bank and investors are the most important aspect of your project. Without them, there is no project. Form a committee or have a meeting with the interested parties and important figures in the project. Review all the information and make an informed decision on which proposal to go with.

Chapter Fifteen

INCENTIVES

PART 1:

OFFERING LOCAL TAX INCENTIVES

OFFERING LOCAL ECONOMIC INCENTIVES

Offering incentives can be one of the key things you can use to attract both outside investment and/or local investment. There are many pros and cons to offering incentives.

Offering incentives can put your project on the top of the pile when it comes to working with outside or local investors. There are many investors, developers and so on that will not even work on a project in a community if there is no economic incentive. In many cases, there is a community just down the road that is willing to offer these packages. These projects seem to be a more attractive opportunity for these people. As much as it seems a bit harsh, if you are not playing the incentive game, you may be overlooked. Unfortunately, in some cases, the public does not understand the idea of an incentive. In those cases, a good explanation is necessary to ensure there is as little backlash as possible. Take the time to explain the simple fact that whatever type of incentive, there would be no hotel and no future tax revenue without it. Not to mention the jobs and collateral revenue and tax revenue we highlighted in the lesson on the impact of a hotel. Let us get into the types of incentives there are out there to offer.

There are many types of economic incentives out there. Some states do not allow certain types but for the most part, all communities have an opportunity to incentivize in some manner.

The first type and most attractive to outside investment is the up-front incentives. These incentives essentially offer the investors an opportunity to put less of their cash in the project. In most cases, these up-front, cash incentives are paid back, plus interest with the real estate taxes each year for a numbered amount of years. I have seen markets offer as much as 30% of the total project as an up-front incentive.

For simple math purposes, this is how they may work:

If you have a $10,000,000 hotel project that will have a tax bill of $250,000 per year, an up-front tax incentive of $3,000,000 (in the case of 30%) at 3% interest, it would take about 15 years to pay off. This scenario would net the community over $730,000 in interest over that time (rough math). If you take into consideration all the other collateral revenue it is not a terrible deal.

The next type is the pay-go incentive. This incentive is essentially an ongoing tax discount. I have seen these incentives be a full tax rebate each year. I have also seen these incentives by a percentage of the taxes returned each year. These incentives typically do not have an interest factor but each one is different.

For simple math purposes, this is how they may work:

If you have a $10,000,000 hotel project that will have a tax bill of $250,000 per year, a full rebate pay-go would offer 12 Years where the project will receive a tax rebate fully offering a $3,000,000 incentive. In some cases, it can be a percentage. For instance, you may be at a 100% rebate for the first 5 years, then on the 6th year, it will be a 75% rebate, the 11th year at 50% rebate, and so on. The combinations are endless.

Another potential incentive is to help with land, connection fees, permit fees, land prep costs, and so on. These are less attractive but can do the job as well. It all depends on how attractive your study is to a potential developer and/or investors.

The key is the keep an open mind and do your research. In addition to these incentives, most counties or states offer different types of economic incentives that you can use to make your hotel project look even better! Find out and think outside the box!

Chapter Sixteen

INCENTIVES

PART 2:

OPPORTUNITY ZONES

OPPORTUNITY ZONES

Opportunity Zones are a new way for investors to reinvest their money into certain areas across the country with large tax advantages. IF you have an Opportunity Zone in your community, you have an extra edge on attracting investments. Let us go through some details about Opportunity Zones.

HOW DOES OPPORTUNITY ZONE INVESTING WORK?

An investor who has triggered a capital gain by selling an asset like stocks or real estate can receive special tax benefits if they roll that gain into an Opportunity Fund within 180 days. There are three primary advantages to rolling over a capital gain into an Opportunity Fund:

1. Defer the payment of capital gains

2. Reduce the taxes owed by up to 15% after 7 years

3. Pay zero taxes on gains earned from the Opportunity Fund

WHAT IS AN OPPORTUNITY FUND?

An Opportunity Fund is a new investment vehicle created as part of the Tax Cuts and Jobs Act of 2017 to incentivize investment in targeted communities called Opportunity Zones.

WHAT ARE OPPORTUNITY ZONES?

Opportunity Zones are census tract designated by state and federal governments targeted for economic development.

WHAT ARE THE BENEFITS TO INVESTORS?

Opportunity Funds allow investors to defer federal taxes on any recent capital gains until December 31, 2026, reduce that tax payment by up to 15% and pay as little as zero percent taxes on potential profits from an Opportunity Fund if the investment is held for 10 years.

Disclaimer: We are not giving investment advice. This is for informational purposes only. For investment advice, please seek the counsel of a financial/investment advisor and conduct your due diligence.

Chapter Seventeen

WHAT IF NOTHING IS HAPPENING WITH MY PROJECT?

WHAT IF NOTHING IS HAPPENING WITH MY PROJECT?

I would bet I get this call every few weeks or so.
Community leaders that we have worked with on a
HOTEL FEASIBILITY STUDY that have hit a dead end. They
are not getting a callback or the HOTEL DEVELOPER
simply cannot get the project moving! There is always a
different reason. There is always a different hurdle.
NEWS FLASH, there will be hurdles! Do not let them get
in your way!

There are many reasons for a project coming to a stop.
The key is to not let them get in your way. If the HOTEL
DEVELOPER is not holding up their end of the deal, call
another one. Be cutthroat about it! Have an investor
that was going to invest their land, decide they want
money or even worse, more money than it is worth? Tell
them to hit the road and find new land! If any one of
the components in your project feel they have the
upper hand, they could use that to their advantage.
Ensure that everyone is on the same page. No one is
indispensable. The only component of a hotel project

that is indispensable is the demand generators. If you lose your demand, the project is dead and there is not much you can do.

Your hotel feasibility study is only good for two years max! That is not something we dictate; it is what the banks look for so when you get that study you need to hit the ground running!

For more help with specific hurdles, do not forget to join our Facebook Group. You will need the support of your COMMUNITY HOTEL DEVELOPING PEERS!

Chapter Eighteen

WHAT IF MY HOTEL FEASIBILITY WAS NOT POSITIVE?

WHAT IF MY HOTEL FEASIBILITY WAS NOT POSITIVE?

This does happen in some cases and I have also chosen to look at the bright side. You have two options when this happens:

1. Wait until you have enough need and recommission your Hotel Feasibility Study. Most Study Firms do not charge you for the full study if the result is not positive.
2. Look at this as an opportunity to look at alternative options. If a hotel is not the right fit RIGHT NOW, what is?

WHAT ABOUT A CAMPGROUND OR RV PARK?

According to the Business Wire, there are 75 million households in the United States that go camping on a regular basis. Campgrounds have seen attendance rise steadily since 2014. There are lots of potential reasons for this revitalized national interest in camping.

Fun Facts*

Camping is one of the most popular outdoor recreational activities in the United States.

In 2017, the annual revenue of campgrounds/RV parks was estimated at more than $7 billion.

In 2017, consumers spent an additional $2.8 billion on camping equipment.

In 2017, there were more than 42 million camping participants in the US.

HOW TO START A CAMPGROUND OR RV PARK

Here is a simple process to go through when considering these options:

1. What type of campground business you want to start? Popular types of campgrounds are seasonal campsites, tent-only campgrounds, year-round campgrounds, and campgrounds for RVs.

2. Where do you want to have the park? You may be there for many years, so choose a geographic area you are familiar with and that you enjoy. For example, if

you have never seen snow you may not want to open an RV camping park in Montana. Now, it is certainly easier and possibly cheaper to buy an existing RV camping park. Building your means that you need to outfit each RV area to the cost of up to $20,000 per rental space, which adds up quickly. Add zoning and construction permits, with the cost of land and insurance, and expenses can easily run up to more than a million. If you have a dream of building a park, it is important to weigh your options by consulting with real estate firms that specialize in outdoor venues.

3. Do you want a theme? Although it is not necessary, it is a good idea to think carefully about whether you want your RV camping park to have a focus. For instance, some parks cater to business retreats, whereas some others lean toward creating camps that are attractive to groups of children. Thinking this over not only helps inspire you but also shows you more avenues you can market to your target audience.

Here are a few ideas:

- Fly-fishing campground

- Rafting, canoeing, and kayaking campground

- Motorhome only campground

- Swimming campground

- Fitness campground

- Wheelchair friendly campground

- Extended stay campground

- Motorcycles only campground

- Tent camping only campground

- Seniors only campground

- Tiny Homes on wheels campground

- Trains campground for people who love all things trains

- Wildlife rehab campground for people who want to see nature up close while animals are rehabilitated

- Sailing campground for people who want to learn to sail while they are camping

4. Do you have a business plan? Draw up a sound business plan for your campground business. In it, analyze the competition and feasibility of a campground at the chosen location, and include a construction and development plan to develop the physical part of your campground business. Also, describe your management and marketing plans, as well as projected income and start-up costs.

5. Register your campground business with your city to obtain a business license.

6. Obtain construction and development permits with the appropriate city or state department.

7. Put a team together to construct your campground business. Some things to consider:

- Develop the landscaping, paving, electrical wiring for RV hookups, plumbing, and a dump station for RVs

- Construct recreational areas such as swimming pools, picnic areas with tables and fire rings, game rooms, a bathhouse, laundry facilities, and an office

During Construction:

8. Build a fully responsive website for your campground business. Include information about your campground and the area with photos and suggestions for activities. Also offer an online reservation where guests can book the dates they want to visit. Write to websites and organizations that list campgrounds to have your campground business added to the list with links to your website.

9. Additional Marketing? Some companies specialize in promoting RV camping parks, and these are worth exploring. By targeting your markets for you via various means, they save time. It used to be enough to have your name in camping guides, but with social media and a much broader market, it is vital to diversify your approaches to keep your park full. If you wish to try marketing your RV camping park yourself, that is doable, too. Join the National Association of RV Parks and Campgrounds to be listed. Develop a social media presence, with beautiful pictures of your park and its amenities.

10. Set the fees for your campground business.

Though starting a campground business may require a significant investment, remember to keep your pricing competitive to attract the maximum number of visitors. 11. Finally, Hire maintenance, and service personnel. Make sure they have experience in the tourism industry, are polite and representative of your business, and are reliable.

IS HOME SHARING A BETTER FIT?

Airbnb ranks No. 1 in the home-sharing market, but travel booking giants Priceline Group Inc. and Expedia are catching up by purchasing companies like HomeAway. Airbnb, based in San Francisco, has a roughly 15 percent share of the global home-sharing market, compared with 12 percent for Expedia, 9 percent for Priceline, according to research by the Susquehanna International Group. Both companies are increasing their efforts because they want to increase their presence in a sector projected to grow 8 percent in 2017 to $34 billion.

Why do some travelers like AirBnB or VBRO?

1. Cost - An Airbnb rental is typically much cheaper than a comparable hotel room. Depending on the

location, in some cases, an entire house can be rented via Airbnb for the cost of a single hotel suite.

2. Living Locally - According to statistics one of the main attractions of an Airbnb stay is to "live like a local". Rather than renting a generic hotel room, most Airbnb guests prefer to stay in a neighborhood and experience the destination the way locals do.

3. Privacy - Airbnb users are not constantly surrounded by hotel guests and staff.

4. Peace and Quiet - Airbnb rentals are typically more secluded and do not suffer from noisy hotel activities such as early morning guest departures, maid service, young children, and traffic.

5. See What You Are Getting in Advance - Unlike a hotel where at best you may see an image of a similar room on their website with Airbnb you get detailed photos and descriptions of the actual premises.

6. Diversity - Airbnb has an enormous diversity of available accommodations, from boathouses, and yachts to lighthouses and castles.

7. The Comforts of Home - Rather than generic hotel rooms Airbnb listings have the homey feel of actual living space (some even have resident pets). Kitchens allow guests who wish to save money on dining out or have dietary problems to prepare their food.

8. Space for Family or Friends - With Airbnb, you can save a lot of money by renting an entire house/apartment/condo for family and friends rather than multiple hotel rooms.

EIGHT THINGS TO CONSIDER BEFORE YOU HOME SHARE:

1. What Kind of Host Do You Want to Be? - There are three main types of hosts out there—those that want to make a few extra bucks with their available space, those who want a stable secondary source of income, and those who want to build a serious home-sharing business that will eventually become their main source of income. The more income potential you desire, the more planning, capital, work, and risk you are going to be taking on.

2. Have Realistic Expectations - You do not just list your unit and then money starts to come in. It takes time to chat with potential guests who ask questions before

they are willing to book. It takes time and effort to earn great reviews. It takes time to check guests in and check guests out. Set the right expectations about time commitment by evaluating how much time it will likely take for you to host.

3. Know Pricing - Even though home-sharing has grown by leaps and bounds, there are still markets that just do not and will not have enough demand to support hosting. Wouldn't you want to know if you are in one of these markets? Get a market report from a data provider. Learn Airbnb recommends AirDNA.

4. Insurance Coverage - Especially if you are renting out your home, your home insurance plan is almost guaranteed not to cover any damage that results from short term renting. Yes, Airbnb's $1M guarantee gives great comfort but if you have some special items or risk factors not covered by their policy, you likely need additional insurance.

5. Remember You Have Neighbors - An angry neighbor could kill your hosting dreams. Noise complaints are the biggest indicator of unhappy neighbors. Check out a

nifty product that can help you prevent and manage noise issues with guests.

6. Get Your Landlord's Okay - Many apartments are not open to short term subleasing.

7. Know Who the Competition - You are not the only game in town, and you have competition. The more you know about them and the better you understand what makes them appealing or not appealing to potential guests.

8. Get all the Essentials for Your Listing - Certain amenities are essential to delivering a great experience. Every unit must have furniture so what should you consider when purchasing furniture? The choice of furniture can be distilled into two things: function and form. You must consider what pieces are important to your guests? What need is it fulfilling?

Source LearnAirBnB.com
Source Airbnb.com
Source vrbo.com

Closing

We hope this book was helpful in your Hotel Development process! If you have any questions about the information or need any help to get started, please do not hesitate to contact me day or night!

For more information, please visit www.coredistinctiongroup.com.

Also, if you are ever in need of developing more housing in your community check out my other company,

Housing and Community Advisors (HCA) at www.housing-advisors.com. HCA can help you with Multi-Family, Single Family, and Senior Housing Market Feasibility Studies.

www.ingramcontent.com/pod-product-compliance
Lightning Source LLC
Chambersburg PA
CBHW070547220526
45467CB00003B/1110